ANGER
MANAGEMENT
Workbook for Teens

30+ Successful activities for helping teenagers to manage mood swings, control angry outbursts and gain self-control

By

JERRY M.

TABLE OF CONTENTS

SNEAK PEEK!

- Cove of Ancient Blessings
- Oasis of Friendship
- Boulder of Sorrow
- Meditation Meadows
- Optimism
- Anxiety
- Contentment
- Self-Doubt
- Mt. Patience
- Sea of Self-Love
- Windy Creek
- Sense of Self Boat
- River of Self-Acceptance
- Volcano of Dormant Rage
- Rain of Harmony
- Will-O Tree
- Forest of Excitement

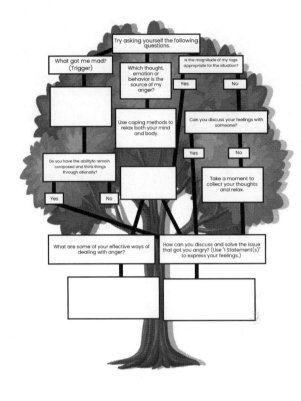

Try asking yourself the following questions.

What got me mad? (Trigger)

Which thought, emotion or behavior is the source of my anger?

Is the magnitude of my rage appropriate for the situation?
- Yes
- No

Use coping methods to relax both your mind and body.

Can you discuss your feelings with someone?
- Yes
- No

Do you have the ability to remain composed and think things through rationally?
- Yes
- No

Take a moment to collect your thoughts and relax.

What are some of your effective ways of dealing with anger?

How can you discuss and solve the issue that got you angry? (Use "I Statement(s)" to express your feelings.)

Leaning into the Anger Roller-Coaster Ride

Anger is a natural emotion. Like every other emotion that exists in this world, anger has many interpretations for all. Some possess enough patience to never explode on others, while there are many who keep exploding on others on a daily basis.

We are not here to play any blame games or deny that anger doesn't have a vital role in everyone's life. Of course, it does! It is just up to us to not let it consume our lives and let it stay in a healthy corner of our lives.

Here, I need to mention a client of mine who had anger management issues since childhood, and he could not let go if someone ever said no to him. It was a harmless habit at first, but it transformed into a problematic issue when he started beating his class fellows for not listening to him.

This workbook is designed for such teens that need to take a chill pill and start working towards redirecting their anger towards something more productive and worth their time.

Just like my client, you can also learn to let your anger go by filling out the worksheets given below. They will teach you to handle your mood swings, control sudden angry outbursts, and exercise self-control. If nothing else works out, we will take you on a journey of Realm of Calmness in the last section because who doesn't love a good fantastical journey?

Now, let's hop on the anger roller-coaster ride, where we will travel through your deepest, darkest moments of anger that bar you from reaching your own Realm of Calmness!

PREPARE TO PRIORITIZE CALMNESS

Before we get into resolving your anger issues and why they make you that mad, it is time to take a minute to reflect on yourself. First of all, learning to control your anger is a big decision and I appreciate you to be willing to take that step!

Now, always remember that only you can decide what you do with your life and no matter what others say or do, YOU have the power to be better and feel better. Take this opportunity to work on yourself by implementing some exercises in your daily life and feel at peace.

Being angry all the time does not help you in anyway, instead, it takes its toll on you by constantly keeping you locked up in your negative thoughts. Your happiness and calmness can only come from keeping your anger at bay and working on channeling it towards something productive.

The only tools you need to embark on this journey are patience, resilience, and boat load of imagination!

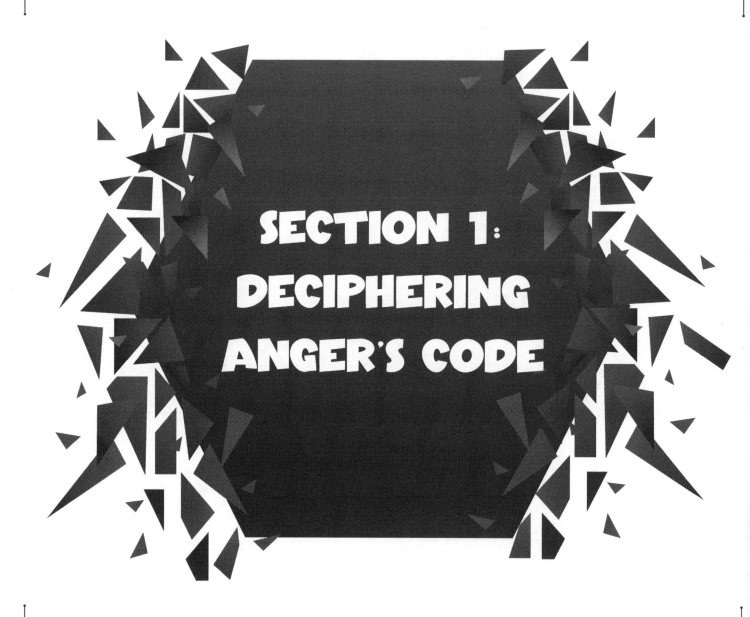

SECTION 1: DECIPHERING ANGER'S CODE

Sometimes, anger sneaks up on you, and you have no idea where it is coming from or why. Nevertheless, there is always a root cause, and by looking for hidden reasons, we can make our lives a thousand times better.

Let's start with figuring out where your anger stems from.

DOING A SELF-ASSESSMENT OF ANGER

No one can know you better than yourself. So, the best bet against controlling your anger is to assess yourself first. You can easily find out about your patterns and shortcomings by following the prompts given ahead and answering truthfully. The only question is, are you ready?

Directions:

1. Check your anger management skills by answering the following prompts.
2. Give yourself a rating of S (Strength), O (Okay), or N (Needs improvement) for each ability.
3. Next, answer the questions given below the prompts.

Benefits:

This activity will help you with:

- Understanding yourself better and your emotions.
- Figure out patterns of behavior.
- Clearly list any shortcomings that need improvement.

_____ I am a sympathetic person.

_____ I don't lose my temper easily.

_____ I don't lose my temper quickly.

_____ I immediately overcome my anger.

_____ I try not to argue with other people.

_____ When I am angry, I speak in a positive manner.

_____ I'm not too bothered by little things.

_____ I don't usually or almost never yell when I'm mad.

_____ I am considerate of other people.

_____ I have an optimistic outlook about myself.

_____ I have never been in trouble for being angry at school.

_____ When I am angry, I try to keep my mouth shut.

_____ When I am furious, I utilize coping mechanisms to help me calm down.

_____ I can control my emotions and make good choices when I am angry.

_____ When I feel myself becoming upset or annoyed, I force myself to refrain from getting into an argument with other people.

_____ My anger has no effect on how I get along with my friends or with other kids.

_____ When I am frustrated, I am able to seek and take support from others.

_____ I never become violent when I'm angry; I don't slam doors, toss objects, strike, kick, or act out.

_____ I never fight with my family or cause a disturbance at home because I'm angry.

_____ Once I've let out my anger, I never feel any remorse, grief, annoyance, or frustration in myself.

Which two of the actions mentioned above would change your life the most if you worked on them?

_____

How can you better regulate your anger? Write your thoughts on the matter.

_____

ACTIVITY 2

Learning About Healthy and Unhealthy Anger Management

There are many ways to express your anger or explosive feelings, but choosing the best way to convey your feelings or thoughts is up to us.

You can see a clear difference between healthy and unhealthy anger.

A COMPARISON OF HEALTHY AND UNHEALTHY ANGER

HEALTHY ANGER	UNHEALTHY ANGER
Straightforward, assertive	Indirect and mocking
Takes responsibility for the mistakes	Concentrated on pointing errors
A firm, clear tone of voice	The abrasive tone of speech
Retains personal space	Obstructing or preventing exits
Emphasis on one's own wants and needs	Focused on laying blame elsewhere
Expresses emotions when responding	Not thinking before responding hastily

DOING A SELF-ASSESSMENT OF ANGER

Do you see the difference? Now, it is time for you to express your healthy and unhealthy anger instances. Write down any latest experiences that come to your mind when you showed restraint or went berserk on others.

Directions:

1. You have learned about healthy and unhealthy anger. Now, write a few examples of when you experienced both.

2. Think about your recent behavior and identify moments when you used your anger in a healthy way and situations when you reacted in an unhealthy way.

Benefits:

This activity will make you aware of the following:

- Your general approach to handling anger.
- Your degree of control over the relationship of actions and emotions in relation to anger.
- Your ability to use anger as a weapon for building confidence and gaining trust.

My Instances of...

Healthy Anger	Unhealthy Anger
_____	_____
_____	_____
_____	_____
_____	_____
_____	_____
_____	_____
_____	_____
_____	_____
_____	_____
_____	_____
_____	_____
_____	_____
_____	_____

UNHEALTHY PRACTICES VERSUS COPING ACTIONS

It's possible that your actions or words might be influenced by anger before you even become aware of how you are feeling. To control your anger, it is necessary to recognize the indicators that tell you how you really feel. Use this worksheet to help you recognize problematic anger behaviors by ticking the boxes next to each action that relates to you. Then, list a substitute action or coping mechanism you may use whenever you catch yourself about to engage in an unproductive action.

Directions:

1. There are a few unhealthy or poor actions listed on the left side. Read through them and mark a tick on each behavior you experience in your angry state of mind.

2. Next, mention anything that has helped you in front of each behavior in the "Alternate Coping Actions" section. It can help you list items or behaviors that help you the most.

Benefits:

Benefits of this exercise include:

- Becoming aware of the intensity of angry behaviors.
- Understanding the physical effects of anger on your body.
- Make a list of potential helpful activities or behaviors that can take the edge off your anger in the worst times.

Poor Behavior	Tried This?		Alternate Coping Action
	No	Yes	
I make a sour expression.			
My face becomes flushed.			
I clench my fists.			
I start insulting others.			
My mind becomes blank.			
I start trembling.			
I begin to breathe heavily.			
I start yelling or increasing my voice.			
I punch things or surfaces.			
I start arguing with people.			
I stop talking or shut off.			
I start pacing around.			
I obsess over the issue.			
I begin to cry.			
I feel nauseous.			
I begin tossing objects.			
I begin to sweat.			
I feel warm.			

UNHEALTHY PRACTICES VERSUS COPING ACTIONS

Anger can be a confusing emotion, especially when you cannot find why you are angry or for what purpose exactly. It is always better to break down the issue by analyzing each moment to see what ticks you off and why. This activity will help you achieve just that.

Directions:

1. Look back at an instance when you displayed anger in full force.
2. Use the questions given ahead to break down the whole situation and analyze where it all went wrong.

Benefits:

This exercise will help you with the following:

- Dig deeper into the reasons for your anger.
- Allow you to find answers as to why you became angry and how you can stop yourself from reaching the same level again.

Time and Date	
Situation What happened right before you got angry?	
Feeling "Hot" and Angry What ideas, pictures, or memories crossed your mind?	
Emotional and Physiological Sensations What did you initially experience?	
Substitute Viewpoints Can you think of any thought(s) that could have helped you calm down?	

ACTIVITY 5

WHEN ANGER BECOMES A PROBLEM FOR ME

Anger is a difficult emotion to manage, and it is frequently caused by other emotions such as anxiety, grief, and disappointment. When anger spirals out of control and threatens to hurt you or those around you, it could pose a problem. Your answers to the questions on the worksheet are going to help you understand more about your anger management problems.

Directions:

1. Answer the questions given ahead by placing a tick mark on "Yes" or "No".
2. Try to answer the questions as truthfully as possible.

Benefits:

This exercise will help you with the following:

- This activity is here to help you realize the adverse effects of your anger on yourself and others around you.
- It is also a great way to identify the extent of your anger and how far you are willing to go. Being aware is the first step in bringing positive changes in your behavior or personality.

Question	Yes	No
Has your anger harmed any of your relationships?		
Do you deal with illogical or erratic thoughts all day?		
Do you ever feel like you get your way when you're angry?		
Do you consider yourself safe or comfortable when you are angry?		
Do you get verbally or physically angry towards others, pets, or objects on a regular basis?		
Do you sometimes lose control when you are angry?		
Do you experience anger at least five days a week for most of the day?		
Have you ever experienced physical, psychological, or sexual abuse?		
Do you believe that anger is easier to manage than other emotions?		
Do you have difficulty controlling your impulses?		
Do you find it difficult to manage your anger?		
Do you experience anger three or more times each week?		
Do you also deal with other emotions, such as discouragement or anxiety?		
Is the degree of my anger inappropriate considering the situation at hand?		

DECIPHERING BUTTON-PUSHING TACTICS

An individual's anger triggers are actions or remarks that provoke anger or agitation. These remarks can be directed towards you, someone else, or something else. You may better organize your ideas on what specifically aggravates you and how to prevent letting others push your anger buttons by using this worksheet.

Directions:

1. Answer the questions below by thinking back to the last time you felt really furious.
2. Once you have your answers, assign each trigger a color and fill in the shirt buttons given below it from start to bottom.
3. Arrange the colors according to what aspect of a situation or a person makes you angry the most.

Benefits:

You may have heard about setting your priorities straight, but now you need to set your triggers straight. They will allow you to pinpoint who or what aggravates you most in life. Once you know the number of triggers and their impact, it will be easier for you not to let these things push your buttons.

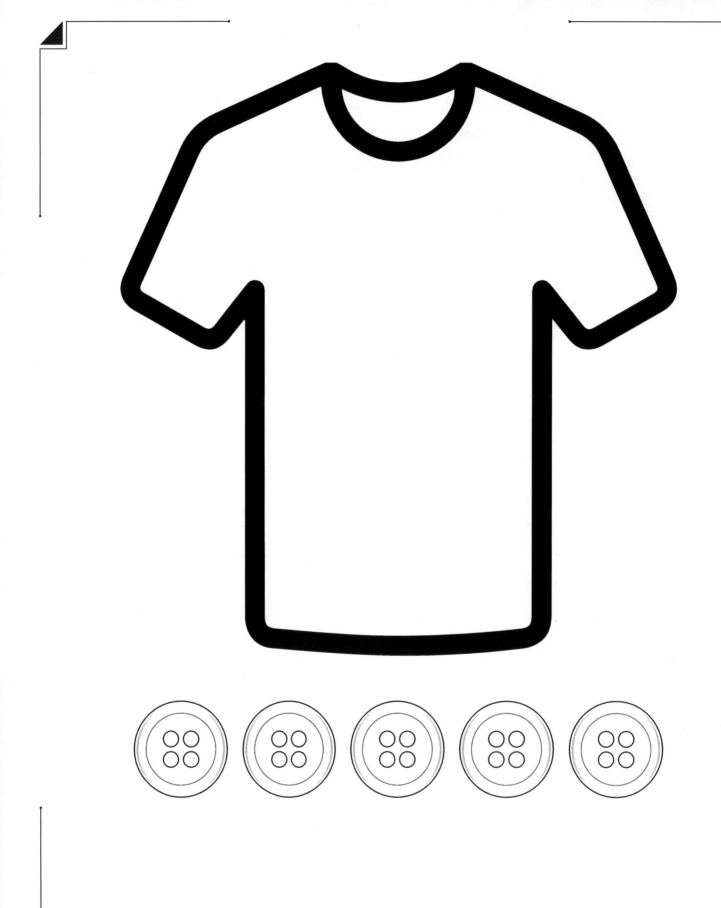

Who were you mad at?

What did they say or do that "pushed your buttons"?

Where did this take place?

What time did it occur?

Why did they act in this way?

Why did that make you angry?

How did you react to the situation?

How will you avoid letting them press your buttons the next time?

Section Notes

SECTION 2: Reigning Back My Mood Swings

Being a teenager means you are bound to have mood swings from time to time. It's normal to go from feeling too much to nothing at all in a matter of seconds. As you know, they can only be controlled but never eradicated from you, so it is best to work on your self-control to feel a little better. Over time, you are sure to develop resistance to not act on your impulsive mood swings.

My Mood Swing Reaction Scale

A person's emotional responses might sometimes overpower them. Sometimes, people may suppress their feelings and show no reaction at all. People that are resilient are conscious of their responses and are capable of using the proper self-care techniques. Do you understand how you are responding to the circumstances at hand? If not, try this test.

Give the situation a stress score.

Not stressful at all	Low stress	Moderate stress	Significant stress	Overwhelming stress

Assess your level of anger.

Not bothered	A little upset	Distraught	Overwhelmed	Unable to handle it

Compare the outcomes. One or more of the following methods may help you adjust your reaction time and avoid overreacting or underreacting.

Under-reaction	Over-reaction
Remind yourself that experiencing emotions does not imply weakness.	You may help yourself calm down by using relaxing practices.
Find out what emotions are hiding inside and how they are impacting the way you act, sleep, and develop relationships.	Find out what made you so unhappy and address it. Had it been a while since your last meal? Was this morning busy? Was that anything someone said? It can be easier for you to control your triggers if you are aware of them now.
Thinking of your feelings as messages is a great way to work on accepting them. No emotion is "good" or "bad." They provide us with useful information and are impartial.	Keep an eye out for all-or-nothing words such as "always" and "never." Words like this encourage "worst-case scenario" thinking.
By meditating, you may learn to sit with your emotions and recognize them without criticizing them or trying to make them go away.	Remove yourself from the situation in order to gain a clearer perspective. What may someone else think about it?

Directions:

Now, it is your turn to see which category your reactions fall under.

1. Write down any reaction that you feel does not belong in the normal category and should be written down on the worksheet below.

2. Check mark the boxes of "Under-reaction" or "Over-reaction", whichever is most appropriate.

3. Next, add your reasons for why you feel your reaction falls under the category it does.

Benefits:

This activity will bring you a clear understanding of your reaction pattern. If you under or over-react at times, it will give you the opportunity to go into detail about why. It will also make sure to understand the importance of behaving appropriately in difficult times.

The Situation	Under-Reaction	Over-Reaction	The Reasons

ACTIVITY 8

FLUCTUATING DAILY EMOTIONS

Emotions never stay static. Sometimes they are in such abundance that it can be difficult to rein them in, and other times, even the biggest news cannot make you care one bit.

Use this activity to vent your daily emotions, positive or negative.

Directions:

1. You see some prompts on the worksheet ahead.
2. Read them and answer accordingly. One column is for "Positive Emotions", and the other is for "Negative Emotions".

Benefits:

Processing emotions in a timely manner can bring many positive changes in your life. Use this exercise daily to leave the emotions of the day where you encountered them instead of dragging them along through the week.

A POSITIVE FEELING I EXPERIENCED TODAY WAS...

[ ]

WHO OR WHAT SETTING CAUSED ME TO FEEL THIS WAY?

[ ]

WHY DID I REACT THAT WAY?

[ ]

HOW DID OTHERS BEHAVE?

[ ]

HOW DO I CONTINUE TO HAVE DAYS LIKE THIS?

[ ]

A NEGATIVE FEELING I EXPERIENCED TODAY WAS...

[ ]

WHAT HAPPENED TO MAKE ME FEEL LIKE THIS?

[ ]

WHY DID I REACT THAT WAY?

[ ]

DO I FEEL BETTER BECAUSE SOMEONE HELPED ME OR BECAUSE I USED A COPING SKILL?

[ ]

WHAT WILL I DO TO HELP MYSELF COPE AND GET BETTER IF I HAVE THIS FEELING AGAIN?

[ ]

ACTIVITY 9

SITUATIONAL SELF-REFLECTION

Every situation we encounter is distinct and causes us to feel a variety of emotions. You may feel sad in one instance and mad in another. It is important to self-reflect on what your feelings are at any moment.

Use this activity to vent your daily emotions, positive or negative.

Directions:

Follow the questions and fill out the worksheet as you see fit.

Benefits:

You will learn the art of self-reflection from this worksheet.

What occurred to make me feel like this?

Is it a good feeling?

What can I do to express my appreciation or to make other people feel the same?

Is it an uncomfortable feeling?

Has anything else happened recently to make me feel bad?

I can do a few things to make myself feel better, such as...

Were there any other emotions you experienced?

- [ ] Embarrassed
- [ ] Scared
- [ ] Excited
- [ ] Confused

- [ ] Happy
- [ ] Frustrated
- [ ] Disappointed
- [ ] Other: _____

- [ ] Angry
- [ ] Nervous
- [ ] Jealous

BEING A VOICE OF REASON

Everyone needs some sort of guidance to know what they can be. You need to learn to internalize this key feature that will allow you to think through your actions before acting on them.

Directions:

1. Write down your previous anger moments when you couldn't control your anger.
2. In the next column, write down your well-thought reasons for why you behaved in that manner and what you could have done better.

Benefits:

This activity will allow you to practice your Voice of Reason. It will make you become your own reasonable guide by looking at facts before acting aggressively in the future.

ANGER MOMENTS	VOICE OF REASON

Section Notes

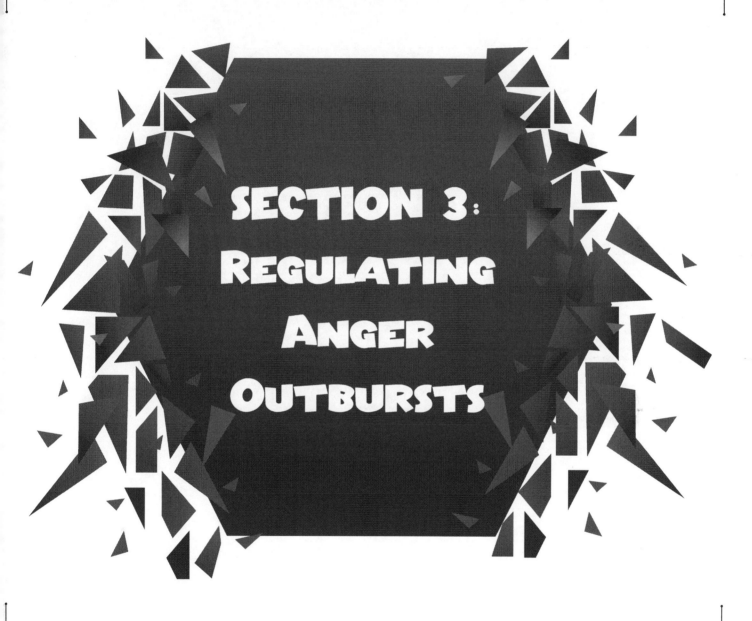

SECTION 3: REGULATING ANGER OUTBURSTS

Anger outbursts happen when you keep things bottled up for too long. If you are ready to leave them behind, the first step is to acknowledge everything that is pulling you down. Once you learn to open up, you will feel much lighter and happier. Easier said than done, right?

Let's start small and get to know your outbursts more intimately. Who knows where it will lead us?

MY RAGE RESPONSES

Rage can be an ugly emotion when it comes out in full force. Let's see how ugly it gets for you. See each response and see how far your rage can go with minimal pushes from people in your surroundings.

Directions:

1. You will find a number of prompts of common anger outburst behaviors that most people exhibit in their aggression.
2. Answer with a tick mark on any one option out of **"Never"**, **"Sometimes"**, or **"Often"**.

Benefits:

This activity will teach you to identify your negative and positive responses that you display in your most extreme state of anger. If you are capable of stopping yourself in the 'heat of the moment,' you can do anything.

Mark the box next to how frequently you exhibit these actions when you're irritated, upset, or furious.

	NEVER	SOMETIMES	OFTEN
Cry			
Hurt myself			
Shout or yell			
Ran away from a situation			
Say hurtful or rude things			
Negatie posts on social media			
Cursing or swearing			
Aggression or harmig others			
Backtalk, disobedience, or arguing			
Sarcasm, imitation, or making fun of others			
Ridicule, name-call, or criticize other people			
Slam doors, smash, or otherwise ruin stuff			
Threaten or retaliate against others			
Give snide remark about others			
Stomp your foot, clap your hands, or pace around			
Close off ignore or decline to take part in anything			
Eye rolling, stairing, or making impolite gestures			
Push, punch, strike, or kick objects or other people			
Maintain composure			
Be in control of your cravings or impulses			
Try a coping strategy to calm down			

ACTIVITY 12

TRACKING MY ANGER LEVEL

Anger can be tricky to understand or get around when you don't know the extent of its implications on your mind and body. Practice this activity whenever you start feeling angry. It will allow you to rate your anger and consequent reaction beforehand.

Directions:

Follows the questions on the worksheet ahead and answers accordingly.

Benefits:

Tracking your anger in self-examination is far more likely to instill the right responses because it gives you time to think about your actions and their results.

Time and Date	
Trigger What occurred right before you became angry?	
Fury Level Select a value between 1 and 10, with 1 representing no anger and 10 representing intense anger, to indicate how furious you were.	☐ ☐ ☐ ☐ ☐ ☐ ☐ ☐ ☐ ☐ 1–Not Upset　　　　　　Extremely Angry–10
Reaction What was your response?	
Rating of Reaction Using a scale of 1 to 10, rank your response, with 1 representing the worst possible response and 10 the best response.	☐ ☐ ☐ ☐ ☐ ☐ ☐ ☐ ☐ ☐ 1–Not Upset　　　　　　Extremely Angry–10
In the Future How will you handle your anger differently the next time?	

ROADMAP OF MY ANGRY REACTIONS

When you begin to feel furious, there are various warning indicators that you experience in your body. If you recognize these symptoms, you may use coping mechanisms to control your anger before it becomes out of control.

Directions:

1. Here, you see a few blank road signs. Use each sign to write and draw which indicators tell you that you are gradually coming close to exploding soon.
2. Start from the left side and write which indicators tell you that an explosion is happening soon.

Benefits:

Roadmap of My Angry Reactions will allow you to mention each and every sign that comes in your journey, from feeling normal to feeling red with anger. It will help you recognize your triggers and take precautions whenever they next show up.

AGITATION FLOW CHART

Agitation, like anger, can strike anytime. It is best to focus on it by going through the steps of how and why it angered you so much. Let's make a flow chart that encompasses where your anger and agitation started and where it will end.

Directions:

Follow the flowchart starting from the top and getting to the bottom of it.

Benefits:

This activity will allow you to let you filter your thoughts by focusing on each aspect of your anger, one at a time.

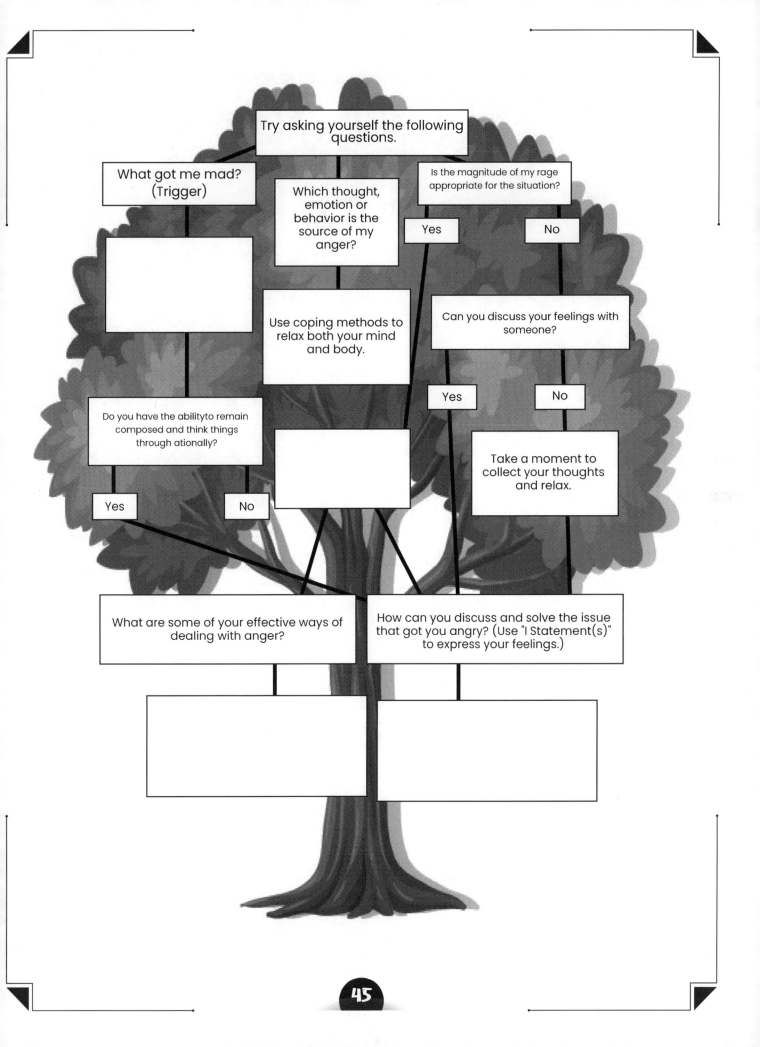

Try asking yourself the following questions.

What got me mad? (Trigger)

Which thought, emotion or behavior is the source of my anger?

Is the magnitude of my rage appropriate for the situation?

Yes

No

Use coping methods to relax both your mind and body.

Can you discuss your feelings with someone?

Yes

No

Do you have the ability to remain composed and think things through ationally?

Take a moment to collect your thoughts and relax.

Yes

No

What are some of your effective ways of dealing with anger?

How can you discuss and solve the issue that got you angry? (Use "I Statement(s)" to express your feelings.)

ACTIVITY 15

MY ANGER ALARMS

Anger is a universal emotion, yet everyone expresses it differently. Some people may become quite silent, while others may become extremely loud and violent.

Alarms serve as indicators that something negative is about to happen. It is up to you to be aware of what changes you go through, whether physical or mental that brings you closer to expressing a violent outburst. This worksheet will help you plan ahead for your angry moments and work on feeling better next time.

Directions:

Answer the questions given ahead.

Benefits:

By completing this worksheet, you may learn to recognize the warning signs of anger and take steps to manage your emotions. It will also help you measure your reactions and explore techniques to maintain composure in the future.

PSYCHOLOGICAL INDICATORS

What goes through your mind when you are feeling angry?

How does your body react to anger?

How do you behave when you are furious?

POSSIBILITY TO REACT

How do you usually respond when angry?

Do you ever feel out of control when you are angry?

How do others respond to your anger?

How violent are your outbursts when you get angry?

When you are furious, do you consider how severely your actions impact you and others?

MAINTAINING YOUR COMPOSURE

How do you maintain composure and resist being angry?

How will you maintain composure the next time you find yourself in a heated situation?

When you start to feel angry, what will you tell yourself?

WHICH TRIGGERS LIGHT THE MATCH?

Triggers can be very upsetting, and they tend to make you mad in an instant. Lighting the Match may not be in your control, but controlling your response to them may be. Use this activity to identify your triggers and explore their possible solutions.

Directions:

1. Write about your anger triggers on the provided lines.
2. Give their possible solutions after you have identified your triggers.

Benefits:

This activity is your way of recognizing your anger triggers and develops personalized solutions to manage them effectively. It empowers you to take proactive steps in diffusing these triggers on time.

The Triggers that Make the Match Light...

_____

_____

_____

_____

Water Bucket of Possible Solutions...

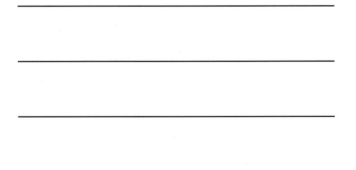

_____

_____

_____

_____

PORTRAYAL OF MY VOLCANIC ERUPTION

Anger is frequently compared to volcanoes and eruptions because it does work similarly, especially in people prone to express violent or intense outbursts. It feels similar because we tend to keep our feelings to ourselves, and most of the time, that emerges in the shape of pent-up frustration that ruins your and others' mood in an instant.

The Portrayal of My Volcanic Eruption will allow you to safely process everything you feel at this moment and sort out the reasons that will most likely make them erupt violently.

Directions:

1. First, take a moment to think about which other feelings describe you best when you are getting angry at something.
2. Write down everything that you feel in the space below the volcano.
3. Next, write down the reasons on the right side of the volcano which makes you boil at any moment.
4. Start from the bottom of the volcano to its top. Write reasons according to their intensity till going to the top that makes you angry the most.

Benefits:

This activity will aid you in penning down all negative feelings that are swelling inside you. It will also help you with finding reasons for your violent outbursts before they burn you.

Section Notes

SECTION 4: LEARNING THE ART OF SELF-CONTROL

Control comes from feeling empowered enough in your own strength that you believe everything can be alright. It is not about just controlling powerful and intense emotions like anger but feeling confident in you. It also means that you can admit when you are fine and when you need help.

In this section, we will look into activities that focus on providing you with more self-control on your emotions, thoughts, and behaviors.

ACTIVITY 18

STAGES OF SELF-CONTROL

Self-Control does not develop in a day or two. It needs you to work on it consistently for days before seeing any kind of result. It is up to you to go through each stage with patience and endure the issues you face on the way.

These are the stages that one must cross to learn self-control, they are:

Stage 1: **Pre-Consideration** Oblivious to the issue	**Stage 2:** **Consideration** Aware of the issue and the intended improvement	**Stage 3:** **Planning** Making plans for implementation
Stage 4: **Process** Demonstrates desirable behavior	**Stage 5:** **Continuation** Supports behavioral transformation	**Stage 6:** **Reversion** Relapse into previous habits

If you wish to build self-control, you must endure the crushing weight of your actions and learn to carry them gracefully through life. Let this activity help you with that.

Directions:

1. Examine each step of transformation and consider which stage you are now experiencing.
2. Next, start responding to the questions at the point where you find yourself right now.

Benefits:

Self-control develops through bringing change. If you start working on changing yourself for the better, you will:

- Learn to accept new things in life.
- Let go of the past and any subsequent emotions you may have attached to them.
- Embrace the idea of working hard to get desired results.

Stage 1: Pre-Consideration

At this time, you might not recognize that there is an issue or a need for improvement. During the first step, you may dismiss, neglect, or deny the issue.

Are there any possible problems in your life that you tend to dismiss, ignore, or deny? If so, could you explain?

Are you or anybody around you suffering as a result of your actions?

Stage 2: Consideration

You are informed that you could have an issue at this point. You will also think about strategies to alter your behavior to solve the issues at hand.

What are the advantages of undergoing change?

What are the drawbacks of implementing a change?

What feelings are you experiencing right now?

Stage 3: Planning

At this point, you have committed to changing your behavior within the next month.

What should you do to start making a difference?

```



```

What is your motivation for making a change?

```



```

How do you plan to handle any worries and uncertainties?

```



```

Stage 4: Process

In this step, you finally put all of your planning to use. You can create a difference by figuring out a suitable procedure.

What is your strategy?

```



```

Is there a support structure in place to assist you in taking action? If so, then who is it?

```



```

What obstacles do you anticipate, and how do you plan to get around them?

```



```

Stage 5: Continuation

You are regularly sustaining the adjustments you planned and implemented throughout this stage.

Which modifications to your action plan did you find to be the most useful?

Which modifications to your action plan did you find to be the least useful?

Which modifications to your action plan did you find most challenging?

Which modifications to your action plan did you find to be the least difficult?

Stage 6: Reversion

Everyone is susceptible to relapses. Relapses are merely a necessary part of the healing process, not a sign of failure.

What do you think caused your reversion?

What lessons can you take away from it?

What is your strategy for getting back on track? Explain in detail.

WHAT DID I DO WITH MY ANGER?

This worksheet can assist you in identifying the things that make you angry, whether at yourself or someone else. Triggers are easy to find, but the real head-scratcher is the part where you must decide which response is more appropriate.

So, let's practice how you will respond to difficult situations!

Directions:

1. Make a list of the things that aggravate you on the worksheet.

2. The next step is to come up with an answer for each thing on your list that either deals with the situation assertively or lets it go.

3. Add a tick mark to the approach that, in your opinion, works best in that circumstance, whether it's letting go or being assertive.

Benefits:

"What Did I Do with My Anger" is an activity that will allow you to compare your responses before acting on your anger impulses. It helps you to work on thinking about alternate actions you can take for each and every issue and react accordingly, fostering personal growth and effective anger management.

Trigger	Respond Assertively	OR	Overlook the Issue
Who or what makes you angry? Make a list of potential triggers below.	How would you behave assertively using assertion strategies?	OR	Is there anything you would say to yourself if you wanted to control your anger and move on?
	Pick this option? ☐	OR	Pick this option? ☐
	Pick this option? ☐	OR	Pick this option? ☐
	Pick this option? ☐	OR	Pick this option? ☐
	Pick this option? ☐	OR	Pick this option? ☐
	Pick this option? ☐	OR	Pick this option? ☐
	Pick this option? ☐	OR	Pick this option? ☐
	Pick this option? ☐	OR	Pick this option? ☐
	Pick this option? ☐	OR	Pick this option? ☐

EFFECTIVE ANGER CONTROL METHODS

We all experience anger, but occasionally people may express it excessively. These situations call for the learning and application of anger control skills. You may test out potential anger management strategies using this worksheet, debate them with others, and come up with your own strategies.

Directions:

1. Techniques for controlling one's anger can be discussed or generated in brainstorming sessions; note them in column 1.
2. When you feel anger rising, try some of these strategies and mark them off in column 2.
3. Finally, list the anger management strategies that worked well for you.

Benefits:

The Effective Anger Control Methods will help you by listing some anger management techniques that can make you better at self-control and not let anger take the lead every time.

Potentially Effective Methods	Did You Try?

Effective Anger Control Methods That Worked For Me

ANGER RECORD-JOURNAL

This Anger Record-Journal is here to help you understand the effects of your anger and how to manage them. Spend some time every day thinking back on instances that made you furious or upset. This can eventually assist you in discovering your anger triggers and constructive coping mechanisms.

Directions:

1. Take 5 minutes each day to reflect on your day and how it impacted your mind and body.

2. At least follow through with this exercise for a week and see the results. It should give you an accurate description of which outcomes are most prevalent in your life and if they need changing.

Benefits:

The Anger Record- Journal will help you with writing down precise moments that made you go out of control. They can help you with learning to recognize the adverse effects and work towards minimizing them in your life.

TRIGGER Why was I angry?	PERSPECTIVE What did I have in mind?	BODY LANGUAGE How did I feel physically?	BEHAVIOR What was my response? How did I act?	RESULT How did things turn out? (For Better or Worse)

Section Notes

SECTION 5: PRACTICE A CALMING ROUTINE OUTDOORS

Cove of Ancient Blessings

Oasis of Friendship

Boulder of Sorrow

Meditation Meadows

Optimism

Anxiety

Contentment

Self-Doubt

Mt. Patience

Sea of Self-Love

Windy Creek

Sense of Self Boat

River of Self-Acceptance

Volcano of Dormant Rage

Rain of Harmony

Will-O Tree

Forest of Excitement

Welcome to the Realm of Calmness. As you can guess right now, it is a fictitious piece of land that embodies everything we must incorporate into our lives. But the question is, how do we get there? We have gone over a lot of things in this book to reach this point, and it is for the sole purpose of getting anger out of your head.

You may not find a physical adaptation of this map, but that is the point; you must make one yourself. Let us tour around this place first and see which activities await us there! Then, we can come to your map of calmness later on.

The Realm of Calmness is a distant land of serenity and peacefulness that you can reach if you just learn to control yourself better. It has everything you need to interact with your content self. It has a Cove of Ancient Blessings that you can go to lock your inner warlock and recognize your innate abilities. On its right, you will find an Oasis of Friendship that sustains your most precious and honest friends in life.

You move a little south to come upon Mount Patience, which holds everything you have kept inside, not to let it erupt like a volcano itself. Down the hill, you come up on Meditative Meadows that harbors the fruits of your patience and endurance. On your way to Windy Creek, you should see a Boulder of Sorrow but be careful! Try not to pass by it to catch the sorrow yourself. Move towards Windy Creek instead that bellows the breeze of soothing nature, taking your worries away with just a gust of wind. These gusts may carry the sound of splashing water to your ears, bringing your attention to the River of Self-Acceptance. It never looks the same, experiencing high and low tides every day, but the least you can do every day is to let it flow.

The River of Self-Acceptance falls into the Sea of Self-Love. Pouring everything in to accommodate the Sense of Self and keeping it a float. The boat passes from battling islands where Island Self-Doubt is constantly at war with Island Contentment and Island Optimism with Island Anxiety, but they never let the other win over completely. Sense of Self Boat reached here after visiting the Volcano of Dormant Rage. It used to spew every other day with lava of rage, but it is dormant now after letting it go. It is now just a reminder of what it used to be before.

Coming back to shore, you see a Forest of Excitement that is buzzing with thrill and noise. It is where all the favorite animals reside. They move in their habitat, just a little distant from Rain of Harmony in the west. This Rain of Harmony only pours when you actually practice harmony and strive to be better at it. Nearby, you will find a Will-O Tree; sit down beside it to take a breath. It will energize your soul while you look at the falling flowers of the Will-O Tree.

Now that you are familiar with the lay of the land, you are free to take up a few activities in the various places it holds. Here are these:

ENJOY THE SCENERY

Sometimes, all you need is to take time and be free. It was no coincidence that we left the story with you at Will-O Tree. Do the same in real life by taking the time to find such a place for yourself. It can be any place that brings you joy and calmness.

DO MEDITATION IN MEDITATIVE MEADOWS

Find a Meditation Meadow for yourself. It may help you when things can get bleak and no other way seems to help you out. Meditation is a breathing exercise that has a lot of variations in bringing you to breathe properly and feel better. Just like Meditation Meadow, find a place that is filled with greenery where you can escape and forget your worries.

ACTIVITY 24

INTERACT WITH PETS AND ANIMALS

Even though the Forest of Excitement is filled with animals, finding a similar forest near you may not be that easy or feasible. If you do, perchance, live near a forest, it is a great place to observe the natural ecosystem (Don't go without supervision).

But don't sweat if you do not find such a place. Your pets are animals, too, and they are more unlikely to harm you anyway. Maybe you can take them along for your adventures in your own Realm of Calmness.

ACTIVITY 25

FEEL THE BREEZE IN WINDY CREEK

Have you ever experienced that kind of day where just one strong gust of wind came out of nowhere and made you smile as if nothing else mattered at that moment in your life? If you haven't, maybe it is time to start doing that.

Go outside on the next windy day, stand in a garden or park, and close your eyes. Just take the breeze in as if you are standing in Windy Creek and there is no one watching you.

ACTIVITY 26

TAKE A SWIM IN THE SEA OF SELF-LOVE

Swimming is a wonderful nice hobby, but what you need most is to find your own immersive hobbies that make your self-love swell and expand. It is only possible by identifying your own interests.

ACTIVITY 27

READ A BOOK

Reading can be very entertaining when it aligns with your interests. Imagine yourself sitting close to the River of Self-Acceptance, with your feet in the water and a book in hand. It could be real you if you choose to find a spot like that yourself. Books stay the same, but readers and their perspectives change. Maybe it is time to do that for yourself.

PLAY WITH FRIENDS

You might be thinking, 'So millennial of him to suggest that!' but it is a great activity that, in my opinion, you need to take up more often. Playing is about interaction and forming bonds that cannot happen with you spending all of your time in books and other indoor activities.

Form your own Oasis of Friendship that stands there for you when everything around is nothing but barren land.

HIKING ON MOUNT PATIENCE

Like Mount Patience needs you to take a difficult hike to reach the top, hiking in real life can turn out to be difficult too. In the same way, it can feel rewarding if you take time to appreciate the amount of work it dumps on you to be successful.

NATURE ART

It is a very simple activity that just needs you to put your skills to good use. 'Art' here does not suggest that you must be good at it, but confident enough to let yourself try it.

Activities such as this one here are meant for you to work on your hidden talents to feel not as angry as before. Who knows where these activities will take you?

All these activities have two things in common: you and your will to try. Anger has taken its toll on you for so long; it is time to let calmness descend on your body and mind. Try all of these activities as you see fit because you are allowed to go through them at your own pace. It is just about doing anything that distracts your anger and allows you to enjoy little things in life. It is time we started to address what else you can do. Do you have any clue? Hint: I mentioned it before.

ACTIVITY 31

DRAWING MY MAP

It's time to make your own map of calmness! Draw any type of map that clearly shows places and activities of your interest.

Map Name: _____

ACTIVITY 32

PROJECT QUELLING ANGER

Now that you have a map, design a list of treasure hunt items/activities that you can find in your map. They will form your anger-quelling checklist, encompassing all things you need to take your anger out in a healthy way.

☐ _____   ☐ _____

☐ _____   ☐ _____

☐ _____   ☐ _____

☐ _____   ☐ _____

☐ _____   ☐ _____

☐ _____   ☐ _____

☐ _____   ☐ _____

Section Notes

TAMING THE FURIOUS BEAST WITHIN YOU

After working in this industry for a long time, I've seen the negative implications of some behavior patterns. This book is my contribution to assisting you in realizing your potential and making a positive difference in the world. All you need is to believe in yourself.

Throughout the Anger Management Workbook for Teens, you have learned about managing your mood swings, controlling your anger outbursts, gaining self-control, and practicing inner calmness.. I certainly hope you will use these activities to calm your anger and behave rationally in the future too.

Here, I would also like to clarify that although this book is a great resource for anger management, it is not a substitute for formal therapy. Talking about your issues in a safe space can benefit you greatly, along with practicing activities that are discussed here.

Hopefully, the furious beast inside you is satiated for now and will remain in reins that will keep it in check.

If you enjoyed the book, do leave a review.

Best Wishes,

Jerry M.

ABOUT THE AUTHOR

Jerry M. is a psychologist with ten years of experience of working with emotionally unstable kids and teens. He has spent a decade of his time in coming up with new ways to connect with young children and teens who feel alone and scared about opening up about their struggles.

Jerry came from a broken family that played a huge part in his life crisis but he turned himself around by not giving up and fighting constantly to build a reputable career.

Made in the USA
Columbia, SC
19 December 2024

49966241R00046